*We are the mirror as well as the face in it.
We are tasting the taste this minute
of eternity. We are pain
and what cures pain, both. We are
the sweet, cold water and the jar that
pours.*

Jalāl al-Dīn Muḥammad Rūmī

BEDRIDDEN TO BUFF

A story of gently healing from chronic pain

by
Pollyanna Darling

LFTW
QLD, AUSTRALIA

LFTW
Perwillowen
Queensland, Australia

Cover design: Fran Johnson-Cash
Cover photography: Adam Styles

First edition
www.pollyannadarling.com

Contents

Prologue

It's early on a chilly morning in April 2023 and I've just pulled up at the boat ramp after sprinting 200m on my standup paddleboard. I feel like I might vomit; my heart is smashing against my ribs, my shoulders leaden. I watch the other competitors pull up, red-faced and panting, hauling their race boards out of the cold murky water.

I won. It's difficult to wrap my head around.

A few hours later, I'm standing on the centre podium, paddle in hand, an official placing a gold medal around my neck. I've won gold in the Australian Over 50s Women's Stand Up Paddleboard 200m Sprint Championship. Later that week I win another gold in a technical race, and a silver in the distance race for my age category. It's like a strange dream, hard to believe that the last five and a half years ever existed.

In 2017, after a series of spinal injuries that led to increasing levels of chronic pain, I herniated a disc in my lower back and spent 6 months doing very little other than lying on my bed. I listened to a lot of podcasts, crocheted endless face washers, felt like a burden to my family, and tried not to think about the future. This book is a collection of stories about the journey from bedridden to buff.

I understand from lived experience, the misery, apathy, depression, fear, resilience, mental strength, and steely hope that is required to live with chronic pain. The days where the pain is unbearable and life seems small and pointless. The days when, for whatever reason, there's relief and suddenly the future opens up a little. And the swing between the two that can be so exhausting.

A pain body is grown; woven together through genetics, experience, injury, thought patterns, trauma, emotions, hormones, and all the complexities of being a human navigating the world. Changing the structure of that pain body, teasing some threads out and leaving others, creating a more supportive structure - it's a process. Since each person is a unique combination of embodied complexity, what works for one person, may not for another. If you're experiencing chronic pain, it's so important to get to know how the weave that is your pain body was made, be astoundingly kind to yourself, and listen with your whole being for the help that will work for you.

This collection of very personal stories is a journey through the creation and unravelling of a pain body. There's a lot missing from this little book because you don't need my entire life story. I'm sharing a few of the experiences that helped to weave my pain body, and my journey to healing. I want everyone to know without a shred of doubt that positive change can, and does happen, sometimes in remarkable and miraculous ways - despite diagnoses and medical history.

In the same way that a droplet of water emerges from a spring in the mountains, joining with other drops, forming rivulets, streams and rivers, passing through waterfalls, eddies, vortices, change is a process. That droplet might eventually reach the ocean, or it might evaporate, condense in the clouds, fall as rain, pass through the bodies of many creatures, wind up back at the spring in the mountains again. Change is not a place you need to get to. It is the incremental journey of ever increasing trust in the process of change itself, in the body, in self, and in life,

What this book isn't

This book is not medical advice and should not be considered such. For medical advice, consult your doctor. I am not a therapist. I am not a counsellor. I am sharing my story and perspective in the hope that it may be useful to you.

ONE - 2016/17

2016 was the worst year of my life.

The previous year I'd had a bleed on the brain in Cusco, Peru from high altitude cerebral edema (a relatively rare condition that mostly only plagues climbers at altitude). I was still recovering from that little adventure when I discovered I was pregnant - unplanned, and unfortunately a Caesar scar ectopic. I was 44 years old, had only one fallopian tube (from a previous ectopic that nearly killed me) and we'd had no accidents. A wildly unlikely pregnancy that resulted in a rare form of ectopic pregnancy where the fertilised egg embeds in the Caesar scar site. On the advice of a specialist, my three older children took turns staying home from school while I waited for treatment, so that I wouldn't be alone in the event the ectopic might rupture and I would die from internal bleeding.

Shortly after the weeks-long, very stressful process of trying to get treatment for the Caesar scar ectopic, my partner had an emotional affair and was fired from his work in dubious circumstances. My heart broke. He moved into the spare room.

It was a relentless shitshow like nothing I'd experienced before, which is saying something given my challenging childhood. I felt incredibly alone, utterly lost and horribly disoriented.

I soldiered on. I couldn't face ending my marriage. I hoped every day that the intoxicating, gentle, hilarious and fun relationship I'd once had would somehow resurrect itself. I had four lovely children and was working as an intuitive life coach from home. My youngest was 6 years old. I was terrified of being alone and not having the support of a partner. I hated the idea of having not just one, but two failed marriages. I didn't want to be separated from my youngest son. I couldn't imagine how I'd support myself and the children alone, or where I'd live or how we'd manage.

Life limped along in the way it does when you turn a blind eye to all the difficult things and try to stay positive and hopeful. The centre of my chest felt hollow. I grew food in the garden, hung out with my children, did my coaching, saw friends - but the hollow deepened. I despised myself for staying in a relationship that had collapsed, for not having the courage to leave. My confidence in my capacity to coach, to parent, to interact with the world slowly dwindled until it was just a whisper.

In 2017, on my birthday, my family paid for me to have a massage. We went to a local spa. We drank hot chocolate and ate seriously good cake. When it was time for my treatment, the therapist began with a foot massage. She sat down opposite me, leaned down and lifted one of my feet. Something pinged in my lower back. It was such an unpleasant sensation that I felt nauseated. But I didn't say anything. I didn't want to make a fuss. So she continued with the foot rub and then gave me a full body massage.

Oddly, when I was leaving the spa, a large woman entirely clothed in ill-fitting black clothes who was talking loudly with friends, reached out and grabbed my arm. She said I was radiant and that she wanted to give me a gift. She reached into her prodigious black bag and drew out a little pouch with a red drawstring. She carefully opened the pouch and held it out to me. It was full of tiny crystals of all colours and shapes. She told me to take three as a blessing. I didn't want to accept, something about the woman bothered me. But again I didn't want to make a fuss, so I took three crystals and we left.

I'd been invited to a party (that just happened to be on my birthday) in a mock medieval castle. Despite the fact that I was exhausted after the massage, and my back felt odd and uncomfortable, I was keen for the party. How often does someone throw a party in a castle on your birthday? Especially in Queensland where we don't even have castles (except this one). So I dressed up as a wench (it was a costume party), took pain relief for my back, and popped my three crystals in my pocket for luck. I was determined to have fun.

I danced all night like a fiend. I don't drink alcohol, but I drank litres of water. It was a steamy summer night and the dancing made me sweat buckets. Because it was my birthday, I got a personal behind-the-scenes tour of the creepy doll collection held in the castle. I felt very special. But some part of me was observing the whole thing from afar. I could see how manic I looked, how hard

I was trying to have fun, how much I was pushing my body. As I danced madly, I could also feel how much other people were enjoying my crazy energy, so I ramped it up. I danced more wildly, over tables, up on a wooden throne. I burned impossibly bright.

At the end of the night, I walked across the castle car park. My whole body felt stiff and awkward. I sat down in the car and my legs wouldn't move properly. I assumed I was tired, drove home, took more pain killers and went to bed.

The next morning I could barely move. Every muscle in my thighs had tensed up and I couldn't make them relax. We were packing for a family holiday 4 hours south of home. I struggled through the prep and the drive with pain relief. During the drive, my back and legs grew stiffer and more sore with every minute that passed. By the time we got to our holiday house, I was gritting my teeth in pain. I staggered to the bedroom and collapsed.

It was a miserable holiday - a week spent whacked out on a round the clock paracetamol / ibuprofen cocktail, and crying in the night because I couldn't find a position that allowed sleep, despite all the drugs. I felt desperately sorry for myself and deeply uncared for. My partner took the kids fishing, swimming, surfing and out to cafes. I lay in the holiday house trying to distract myself by making Spotify playlists and listening to podcasts.

Occasionally I dragged myself to the kitchen for water or food. One night, after hours of no sleep and acute pain, not wanting to disturb my partner, I crawled to the lounge room and lay on the cold, grubby, wooden floor sobbing and wretched.

When we got back home, I sought help from the medical establishment. I had a herniated disc. First it bulged and then the disc of fluid that padded the vertebra ruptured. I was sick with pain -

my skin turned grey, I hadn't slept in well over a week. I couldn't eat. I was a mess. But I knew what was wrong with me and after four days of heavy duty opioids for the pain (which resulted in not sleeping for over a week after I stopped taking them), I started looking for someone who could help me heal.

TWO - 1979

I'm 7. We've just moved into a new house. There are half emptied boxes everywhere. It's topsy-turvy wherever I look, clothes spilling out, pots and pans on the floor of the living room, records bending in boxes in the kitchen, books heaped higgledy-piggledy on chairs. Mum isn't OK. Her eyes are swollen and red every day. She doesn't talk right. There's not much to eat, just white bread from the shop and butter. It's a bit exciting to have white bread because Mum always used to make lumpy dry brown bread. Me and my brother and sister like to pull the white bread crusts off and roll the bread part up into little squashy balls. They're so yummy.

Dad's gone. He went on a business trip right

after we moved. But he didn't come back. Now he lives in a different house in London with a lady I don't know. I don't like her and I don't think she likes us. Dad's drunk every time we see him now.

One day I walk home from school and my grandma is there - my beautiful Hungarian grandma with the warm brown hands. Grandma tells me Mum is in the hospital. That she's not very well and they're going to make her better. That we can go and see her later. When I ask her what's wrong with Mum, she just keeps saying that she's not well. It doesn't make sense.

It's dim in the hospital room. Mum looks like she's lying in a puddle of yellow light. The bed is really high, like a stage. The white sheets are pulled up nearly to her chin. Her skin is a weird colour. She's awake and her eyes are open, but she doesn't say anything. She doesn't move either. She doesn't look like she's hurt.

The corners of the room are full of grey-green shadows. Grandma is there with us. She says come and say hello to your mother. I don't want to. I stand back from the bed in the shadows, so I can be away from everyone. They talk to Mum, but she doesn't answer or move or even blink. My little sister climbs onto the bed and curls up next to her. A nurse comes in and talks to Mum like she's a baby. Grandma beckons me over, but I'm staying right here.

Mum's been in the hospital for weeks. Some days Dad comes to the house and picks us up in his van. It's not even school time and he's drunk. His mum is staying with us now. She's my Welsh grandma with the wrinkly white hands. She's famous for never complaining. Not ever. She also gives Dad beer. I don't want to go with him, but grandma says don't be silly, you have to go to school. Luckily there's lots of traffic and he can't drive fast. I'm still scared. I sit in the front and stare out the side window so I can't see the way the van crosses and uncrosses the white lines.

Sometimes I look over at him; a big lump of clay. His face looks like it's sliding off. A beer smell cloud hangs around him. I feel like I'm holding my breath. My whole body is tight and still, like Mum in the hospital. Dad asks me stupid drunk person questions. I don't answer. I want to be out of the van, away from him.

When we get to school, I jump out without saying goodbye. I can hear him calling for a kiss. Come on Poll, kiss your dad goodbye. I run into the playground without looking back.

I get in trouble at school. I start a game where we run across the playground and jump-slide onto our knees. The one with the biggest grossest scabs wins. You have to pick the scabs to get really good ones. One of the teachers asks me about my parents.

Am I OK? I don't like the way she's looking at me, her eyes all soft and sorry. She says she's trying to help me. I want to get away from her too and go back to the game.

I have a bunch of naughty, funny friends. We break into the stationery cupboard at lunchtime and glue all the textbooks together. It's exciting, giggling in the dark cupboard, doing the wrong thing. When the teacher turns her back, we throw our erasers at the bin and make silly noises. I laugh so much my face hurts and I have tears running down my cheeks. It's hard for anyone else to do their work. Somehow I don't get in any really big trouble. I think it has to do with my drunk father and hospital mother. I sort of want to get into trouble. I'd rather be told off than have the creepy soft eyes and sorry.

Mum comes home. She's been gone for six weeks. I think she's OK. Dad comes over to play LEGO with us sometimes and Mum plays I Will

Survive so loud on the record player that the house shakes. She doesn't come out of the kitchen.

Sometimes we go to Dad's house in London for the weekend. There are posters from all over the world stuck to the walls - a giant scrapbook of people living different lives. People in Paris with fancy hats, American men with cowboy boots leaning on big red cars. More American people in New York smiling and kissing under umbrellas in the rain. Colourful lettering that I want to try and copy. Dad's usually drunk. He forgets to feed us. He forgets our bags. Sometimes his lady is there. He has cats now. They're called Limbo and Milly. Their names make me think of burning in Hell. Our dog, Rover, sometimes comes with us to Dad's. When I'm hungry and Dad's forgotten about dinner, I eat Rover's biscuits. They're very dry. If there's jam in the cupboards, I put jam on them and they're not so bad.

One time Dad says he's going to make chips and cake. He cuts up really old potatoes. Lots of them are very green. He puts them in the oven with the cake. He's very happy with himself that he's making us food. He's excited to be making cake for us because children really like cake. He's drunk and hopeful in a way that hurts in my chest. The chips are soggy when they come out and the cake has a big wet dip in the middle. No one wants to eat them. He says never mind, but I can see that he's upset it didn't work. Now I feel sorry for him, and angry that I have to.

I'm not allowed to do piano lessons anymore. Mrs Follett, my piano teacher, says she can't teach me if all I'm going to do is bang on the keys. She says she's disappointed in me because I was such a promising young piano player. That makes my cheeks get hot. I want to play but I can't.

Everyone is upset with me. Teachers, Mum, Mrs Follett, my Welsh grandma. I'm such a clever girl, why am I not doing my school work? Why won't I play the piano properly? I don't know. The world is tipping over. I keep trying to stand up straight, but I can't.

THREE - 2012

It's a roasting summer afternoon. I've just dropped my three older boys with their dad, my ex husband, after a two hour drive. We did the exchange in a petrol station car park. We're not the only parents doing this. This particular petrol station is convenient for the highway around Brisbane and the car park is capacious. Car doors open and close all over the grey asphalt - kids getting out of one car and into another; Disney backpacks and supermarket bags clutched to their chests as they ferry their belongings between tense parents.

It's so hot. My 1 year old baby is grumpy and grizzling and we now have possibly a four hour drive through Friday afternoon traffic to get home.

I had a pointless and ordinary row with my ex in the car park. I'm rattled and I can feel the tight bubbling of anxiety in my core. I'm a little frightened of him. He can be verbally aggressive. I'm inclined to try and pacify him, but that only makes things worse. He's very angry with me because I left the marriage and broke up his family. I moved with the children to a place a few hours from where he lives, to be closer to friends. I know it's for the best, but whispering in the back of my mind is the idea that I've done the wrong thing and somehow I might lose my children if I can't appease him. I'm so terrified by this that I banish the idea the moment it arises. My stomach is in knots. My heart is pounding unpleasantly in my ears.

I'm driving down the highway towards home. My baby is screaming now. I glance in the rear vision mirror. His hands are balled up, his cheeks red and shiny with tears. There are roadworks everywhere and we're forced to drive at 80km/h. I'm crawling with feelings of guilt so intense that I'm scrunched up around the steering wheel. I couldn't create a smooth transition to their dad for my three older boys. My baby has to endure this drive every two weeks. His howling fills the car. My actions are creating suffering for the people I love the most.

I twist around to try and comfort my boy. He's so hot and miserable; his blue eyes almost swollen shut from crying. I stretch a soothing hand towards his fat little bare foot. He's sobbing in hoarse jerks.

Smash. The airbags punch out. My right arm is hurled towards the roof as my head snaps around to the front; whips back and then forward again. We're stationary. I'm looking out at the crumpled bonnet, steam rising. Who knew airbags were so rough? I wonder if it's a kind of canvas. I look at my right arm which had been across the steering wheel. It's grazed all down the pale tender skin of my forearm. Did the airbag do that? I peer slowly around at my silent baby. 'Are you OK?' He blinks. My whole body feels weird and loose.

There's a brown-haired man tapping on the driver's side window. I wind it down and look at him. Are you OK? he says. I'm going to move my car forward, wait here. He gestures towards the front of my car. It looks like my sedan is connected to the big white ute in front. I watch the man heave himself into the driver's seat. There's a screeching, steamy clunk as the two cars separate. He gets out and walks towards us. I open the door and get out too. My body is heavy and disobedient. I stand next to him. He's telling me that he has a reinforced towbar for pulling drilling rigs, and that's what's caused all the damage. He sounds far far away, but he's so close we're almost touching. We look at the steaming mangled mess that's my car. We look at the back of his ute. It's so white. The reinforced towbar glints greeny-gold in the afternoon sun.

There's a tiny wrinkle in the black rubber mat on his white bumper bar. The man steps forward and smoothes it out with the fingertips of his left hand. He makes a noise that could be satisfaction. He says something to me about no need for insurance because there's no damage to his car and the accident was my fault. He asks me again if I'm OK, if my baby is OK. My baby. I feel like I'm swimming through mud to get to the baby's door. I open it. He's crying again. I unbuckle him and take him in my arms. The man I don't know, whose gleaming towbar has destroyed my car, drives away.

I'm standing in the fast lane of a four lane highway, between the guard rail and the wreck of my car, with my baby in my arms. We're not in

Brisbane's finest neighbourhood. People drive past and yell obscenities at me. I try to think about what I should do. The police arrive. I wonder if they'll sort all this out. They tell me they've called a tow truck. They decide there's nothing here for them to do. They leave. I'm still standing with my baby on the highway. People are still cursing me as they pass - some even slow down to make sure their words land with full effect. It's hot in the sun. We're both sweating. I remember stories about people whose cars have broken down on the highway and how you're not supposed to sit in the car in case it gets clipped by a truck. I press back against the guard rail. It's noisy. The air is gritty with diesel fumes.

The tow truck comes. The driver tells me to get in the cab of his truck. I'm relieved to be away from the sun and the roar of the highway. I cuddle my boy. Once my car is on the truck, the driver asks me where I want to go. I'm over 200km from my home. We don't have a lot of money. I tell him to take us to the nearest smash repairs place. It's not far, but it costs $200 for the tow. The owner of the smash repairs tells me my car is a write-off. He asks me how I'm going to get home.

I stand in the hot dusty car yard trying to work out what to do. My boy has regained his energy and is toddling about in the dirt and car parts. I ring my partner. I tell him what's happened. He says he'll come and get us, but he makes it clear that it's an inconvenience and not what he had planned for his afternoon. Something inside me is shrinking. Guilt prickles my shoulders and the back of my neck. I shouldn't have crashed the car. I shouldn't have turned around. If I hadn't had a fight with my ex and been so stressed out, maybe my baby wouldn't have been howling, maybe I would have paid more attention. If I hadn't left my ex in the first place and moved away, we wouldn't even be doing this stupid drive every fortnight ... I'm hot, my arm hurts and I feel disconnected from everything. Like I'm sleepwalking.

I herd the boy away from the myriad sharp things covered in engine oil and god knows what. The smash repairs people take pity and give us water. They show me a place out of the sun with a chair, but the boy keeps toddling off. I get up over and over in the next few hours. His energy is boundless. I'm just glad he's OK.

I make a million phone calls - to car wreckers, the insurance company - while I chase my baby around the sweltering yard. I ask the smash repairs guy again if he's sure the car is a write-off. He crowbars open the crumpled bonnet and shows me the destruction wrought by the towbar. Slimy fluids coat everything, the radiator is destroyed, bits stick out where they shouldn't. I don't want to think about where we'll get the money for another car.

Hours pass. I herd the boy.

Eventually my partner arrives. He's frustrated. He's been driving in peak hour traffic. He's tired from work. We get in the car and drive in silence almost all the way back home. I don't have anything to say. My mind is blank. The baby doesn't cry.

When we get home, I put my boy to bed. Thankfully he sleeps almost immediately. My partner tells me he's tired and he goes to bed too. I open the fridge. I think I should eat something. Nothing looks appealing. I sit down in the armchair at the end of the long room that is the kitchen. My legs feel crazy heavy, like lumps of damp clay. My heartbeat is whooshing in my ears. I'm shivering. I wonder if I'm in shock. Should I do something about that? I wonder if I'm wrong to think that maybe someone ought to be taking care of me. I had a car crash at 80km/hr after all. But no one is, so maybe it wasn't that bad? The quiet house wraps itself around me as if trying to soothe the hollow place in my heart.

Five weeks later I can't move. My neck is almost completely seized. Getting out of bed is agony. Walking around is agony. I'm taking so many pain killers, I'm stupid with them. I have almost constant headaches. I also have four little boys and a business to run. At the point where tending to anything at all becomes impossible, I realise I need help. I ask around and contact a chiropractor who also does Craniosacral therapy. On the phone, he tells me he's about to retire, but that he'll take a look at me. My partner drives me over there because I'm in so much pain I can't drive. I sit in the waiting room and look at all the chiropractic certificates. I feel guilty again. We'll have to use money we don't have on my treatment.

The chiropractor, who is very kind and gentle,

tells me I should have gone to the hospital when the crash happened. That I have a severe whiplash injury in my neck. He can't understand why I didn't go to the hospital. I don't have any explanation. He agrees to work with me, even though he's retiring. I am deeply grateful to him. His hands ease the agony and I'm able to function again. But the headaches and pain persist.

FOUR - 2017

At the point I started seeking help for my back, I couldn't lift my arms higher than my waist without extreme pain. It hurt to sit, to stand, to lie down. I had X-rays on my neck and spine. The old whiplash injury had fused two vertebrae together in my neck and caused calcification. A straight line where there should be a curve. If only I'd gone to the hospital after the car accident. I had a displaced vertebra in my thoracic spine and a herniated disc in my lower spine. The pain from the herniated disc seemed to have triggered my whole nervous system into meltdown, causing all my muscles to tense up, resulting in pain in the old injuries as well.

The ageing and very knowledgeable orthopaedic doctor who gave me the X-ray results told me there was nothing to be done. I'd just have to learn to live with it. Suck it up buttercup. He also told me that the calcification would likely get worse, and that the issues I had would probably give me pain for the rest of my life. I'd entered his office hopeful that, as an expert on bones, he'd have some kind of solution for me. I left crushed, doomed, written off, heavy with failure.

I felt desperate about not being able to get in the garden. I watched the weeds take over the beds where abundant vegetables had grown. I couldn't walk my German Shorthaired Pointer who was only a year old and full of energy. Without proper exercise she grew more and more neurotic, barking incessantly at everyone who came to the house, even people who stayed overnight. I begged my partner and children to walk her, but they were half hearted about it. She was my dog and therefore my responsibility. We had to give her back to the breeder. It hurt, but I pushed the hurt away. I imagined my Welsh grandmother telling me I was being sensible.

Without exercise, I too was getting neurotic: plagued by miserable thoughts, the future closing out ahead of me, one where I was barely functioning, in a relationship that made both of us miserable, parenting in pain.

If you're a parent and you've experienced chronic pain, you know how hard it can be to remain present and available for your children. Pain makes even the most good-natured humans short tempered and irritable. Children, as wonderful as they are in many ways, can also be very irritating. I felt battered by their boundless energy, constant noise, endless mess, squabbling, running about, need for near non-stop food, and cleaning up after them. By the end of the day, overwhelm took over. I just wanted to eat dinner, lie down in my room, and have some quiet. It was a relief to be alone, but I was eaten up by guilt. I should have been on the other side of the bedroom door with my kids, engaging; and some part of me really wanted that. But I had nothing to offer. All I wanted was relief from the pain.

Over the next few months, I tried every kind of therapy - Bowen, physiotherapy, massage, counselling, acupuncture, talk therapy, eye gazing, homeopathics, naturopathy, energy healing. Sometimes, I'd get some minor relief in the short term, but nothing endured. The pain always came back.

Often the practitioners, believing they knew what I needed, made the pain worse. Sometimes this was because I didn't say anything, even when I knew what they were doing would cause pain, because I didn't want to be seen as difficult, one of 'those' people. Some of them also told me, with a particular head-tilted knowing look, that I was creating the pain myself through the way I was thinking about it; that there was no way that I was 'actually' feeling the level of pain I described. I'd leave those sessions with a growing sense of shame, and sometimes rage. Not only was I making my family's life difficult because I was so incapacitated, but it was also apparently my fault for not thinking about it correctly.

FIVE - 1981

I'm eight or nine years old. We're in my dad's van driving through the countryside. It's a big grey Bedford van with racing stripes down the side. The lary yellow of canola fields whizz past. I know Dad has cider in the back of the van. I'm crossing my fingers and toes that he won't drink it.

He turns around and tells us that he wants to pick flowers for his new wife who's back at home. He says he really loves her. I don't want to hear that. I think maybe he's already drunk some cider because he doesn't pull over on the side of the road. He drives through an open gate and out into a field. Right out into the middle. People don't drive their cars off the road and into the middle of fields. My tummy gets very tight.

He parks the van and gets out. There are a few wildflowers around, but most of the field is long grass. I hear the creak of the back doors opening. I hop out and go to the back of the van. Dad's sitting on the bumper. There are five 1 litre bottles of cider next to him. He's drinking the sixth one. I want to say something, but I'm not sure what. I don't want another drive home where the white line in the middle of the road keeps changing sides. It's scary. My little brother and sister are in the van. I'm the oldest. Someone needs to tell him. The only person who can do that is me.

I take a big breath and say something about him not drinking because he has to drive. He laughs. Don't be silly, he says, it'll be fine. He opens another bottle. When he's drunk most of the third bottle, he stumbles off to find flowers. He's weaving through the grass leaving a swishy trail. He stops here and there to pick flowers. I watch him. I hate him.

I get in the van and close all the doors. I lock them from the inside. I look under the steering wheel. Dad's left the keys. He won't be able to get in. I tell my brother and sister who are 7 and 5 that we can't let Dad in, no matter what happens. That he's drunk and he can't drive like that. They don't like it, but they agree. We wait. We watch him. It's getting on for dusk. I'm glad we're locked in the van.

Eventually, Dad weaves back across the field towards the van. He's clutching a droopy posy of wildflowers in one hand. His jeans are hanging off him, his jumper too loose. He looks like a big drunken idiot. I remind my brother and sister that we're not letting him in.

Dad tries the driver's door. He yanks at it. He's puzzled. He lurches around the van trying the doors. He's telling us to open up. His words are slurry. He bangs on the side of the van with his fist, a metallic pounding. It makes me think of the Tardis in Dr Who. My sister starts to cry. I feel the van closing in around us, it's metal walls protecting us. Dad bangs harder. My brother says maybe we should let him in. No, I say. We can't. He's too drunk to drive.

Somehow, through his drunkenness, it dawns on dad that we've locked him out. He comes around to the front of the van and half climbs up the windscreen. He's sprawled across it like a gigantic clumsy bird. His face is pressed into the glass. His mouth is squashed and I can see the fleshy pink inside of his bottom lip. His saliva smears the windscreen. It's so gross. The hand with the flowers is pressed onto the passenger side of the glass. He's begging me to let him in. My sister cries harder. My brother is pulling at my jumper, telling me I have to open the door.

My brain thumps against my skull. My skin feels hot and tight. I look at this man, my dad, splatted across the windscreen of his van, holding onto his I-love-her flowers, begging to be let in with his voice and his eyes. I hate him, but he's so pathetic. How can I hate someone so useless and feeble? I feel like I'm mean to hate him, but it's boiling away inside. My heart hurts like it's got a rip in it.

He's yelling now. Both my brother and sister are crying and begging me to let him in. They tug at my clothes. Their eyes are wide and wet and pleading in the gloomy light. It's getting dark in the field. My dad crashes around the outside of the van like a wounded bear. It's no use. It's just me. No one will come. No one will help us. I have to let him in. If I don't, who knows how long we'll be in this field. We haven't had dinner. I'm probably going to get in big trouble. And it's cold. He'll get cold. I tried, but I can't change it. I can't do anything. I reach across and unlock the driver's door.

SIX - 2018

It's early Spring. I'm lying on my bed, still. Golden morning light is pouring through the windows. I can feel the sap rising in the fruit trees outside. I watch the magpies poking and tugging at vines and sticks. They're making a nest in the Bunya tree. Spring is bubbling in my blood. I want to dig the compost out of the chicken pen and spread it over the garden beds, sow papaya, tomato, capsicum. I can't. Last week I tried to use the hand trowel to plant a few seedlings. Each movement of my arm sent splintering shockwaves through my body. The next morning I could barely move. It's not worth even trying.

I've found a brilliant podcast called "Seeing White". It's about the history of racism in America.

I'm hooked. Speaking of hooks, I've dug out my much neglected craft bag and started making a crocheted face washer. I feel like a crippled grandma, lying here crocheting. And yet, there's a spacious sweetness to my days. The boys go off to school. My partner goes to work. I listen to two smart, kind men from wildly different backgrounds discussing what it's like to be a black man in modern America. The crochet needle is slim and cool in my hand. Only the smallest movements are required, and a delicate piece of cloth is materialising, row by row. I'm alone. I like it. When the pain in my back becomes acute, I shift positions.

Days pass like this. It's hard to tell them apart. They're punctuated by visits from the boys. My eldest son comes to my room almost every night that he's not at his dad's. He flumps down onto the bed on his belly, cups his chin with his hands, and we chat. I step into his world; one that's opening up before him, a feast of possibility. He'll be 18 this year. I treasure these moments, the love and the laughter, the care he offers me. I hope he's getting what he needs. I invite the other boys to come and chat on the bed, but for some reason they won't. What are they missing out on while their mother just lies in her room, churning out face washers?

I don't have any family here. I came to Australia from England in my early twenties. I was going to travel around the world. Instead, I got married and had children - a story for another day. There's no one to ask for help. We've already called in so many favours from friends in the last year. So it's just me and my partner, muddling along in our dysfunction.

It takes what's left of my mental energy to block thoughts about the future. But they ambush me in quiet moments between podcasts, when I wake up or lie down to sleep. If I leave my marriage, how will I manage? I can't get a job like this. Where would we live? No one would rent to a single woman with four rambunctious boys and two dogs, surely? I can't even pack a box, never mind carry one. Who will help me? Why am I like this? What's wrong with me? Why is my life like this? Maybe if I can get better, my relationship will improve and it will all be OK. Sometimes I notice the way the pain shifts and expands with these thoughts, the way my body collapses in on itself and the heaviness of overwhelm.

But right now, it's Spring and many things feel possible. I've almost finished the "Seeing White" series. I'm getting better at crochet. And I've just landed a wonderful job that I can do from my bed!

SEVEN - 2018

Somewhere in experimenting with all the therapies, a wonderful friend suggested I try Ortho-bionomy. I found Pete who worked not far from our home. He introduced me to the idea of pain as sensation. Not good, not bad, just sensation. I started to have a different relationship with my pain. I spent hours practicing experiencing the pain as sensation. Telling myself it's OK, it's just sensation. Doing that helped me to relax. Helped my nervous system calm down.

The Ortho-bionomy treatments were a nightmare at the beginning. Every session would set off the old injuries. I'd get improvement in my back and terrible pain in my neck. Or improvement in my thoracic spine but then crushing headaches that spread across my face, pinching my sinuses, tightening up all the muscles around my skull.

This freaked Pete out, but he kept trying. He patiently explained to me that my system wanted to change, but that for whatever reason, it would get stuck. Ortho-bionomy works by giving the body the information it needs to create change, to come back into right relationship with itself. My body clearly wasn't listening or maybe it was half-listening. Every session triggered a cascade of other problems. I was a mess.

In the midst of all this, I quit life coaching. That was a huge relief. I lacked the confidence for perky self-promotion, was tired of feeling responsible for people's decisions, and didn't feel like a good example of my own work. I started working online for a global reforestation charity with a team of amazing women. I worked and did Zoom meetings from my bed. I felt supported by the team I worked with and the work felt good to my heart. I was connected to women all over the world through the network the charity ran. I was working in alignment with my values.

Incrementally over many months, with Pete's help, my body began to change. I stopped being terrified of treatments and started to cultivate a tiny seed of trust that change was happening and I was going in the right direction. I was still in pain a lot of the time, but I could go for walks and drive. Some semblance of 'normal' living returned. I was still plagued by daily headaches and back pain, but I was mostly off my bed and that was really something.

Slowly slowly I was able to do more, but my body still felt incredibly fragile - any kind of overexertion and I'd be back in pain for days. Long car journeys, exercise other than walking, lifting anything more than a kilo were all out. Even going in the ocean was a no-no - I was terrified of being rough and tumbled by the waves and having to do days of pain afterwards.

I had ugly, old person, memory foam support cushions on every chair and in the car. I both hated and loved those cushions. They made life doable. They also made me feel geriatric and uncool. But I was doing satisfying work, parenting to the best of my capacity, and feeling a little more hopeful about my life.

EIGHT - 2021

It's late Autumn. The world is manacled by fear, manipulation and sickness. It's close to sunrise. A slender strip of orange is settling onto the horizon. A budding crescent moon dangles low above the shoreline silhouette, pinned to the arc of midnight blue by the brightness of Venus. The water in front of me is dark, moonlight catching the crests of ripples. It's quiet save for the gentle splash of my paddle entering the water. The rest of the club are up ahead, so far ahead, paddling towards markers I can't even see. I push the paddle down into the dark water, pull it out at my feet. Over and over. The board glides under the fading stars as the strip of orange widens.

My neck hurts, my shoulders hurt, my back

hurts. I will pay later. But right now, everything in me is expanding, shifting beyond my skin into the impossible beauty around me. I try to paddle harder but I can't catch the others. Eventually they turn around and come back for me, gifting words of encouragement.

I'm frustrated by how slow I am. I can't seem to get any faster. Everyone tells me it's OK, that all I have to do is paddle and I'll get better. But if I paddle more, there's more pain. In those moments, my body lets me down, straightjacketing me, imposing limits.

Maybe six months before, my ragged second marriage finally imploded. I lost something I thought I'd have until I died - a person I loved deeply who felt like kin at every level. The relationship had been stumbling along, held together with good intentions, children and rare moments of relief for almost four years, but the end was still a shock. Endings can be like that, right? Shocking even when you know in your bones they're coming. In the midst of grief and trying to deal with the old abandonment trauma that ripped through my body and almost destroyed my mental health, I had an idea.

I'd been on a paddleboard once in 2018, for about an hour, in the river mouth at Evans Head. With my back and neck the way they were, I couldn't bike or skate or swim. My family were merrily doing all those things and more. I was terrified of the pain that would come if I went in the ocean and got knocked around by the waves, of hurting myself, of twisting the wrong way, moving wrong and paying for it later. I was living small to avoid future pain. But surely I could do this paddleboard thing? All I had to do was stand up and balance.

From the moment I stood up on the board, I

loved it. Being on the water without a noisy engine, creating forward motion with the limited power of my sore body. Freed from the heaviness of land, flowing with the water. I didn't fall in. I felt comfortable within a few minutes.

Birds stayed put when I paddled past. The russet and white of a sea eagle floated above me, coasting the updrafts. Stingrays darted away in cloudy puffs of sand as I glided over them. Schools of fish shimmered silver in the cool, clear water. There was a blissful smoothness to the motion of paddling and moving over the water.

So in late 2020, despite the fog of grief (or maybe because of it), I decided to join the local Stand Up Paddleboard (SUP) Club. I had no board, no paddle, no leg rope, no real idea how to do it. I didn't even have roof racks on the car to transport a board. Wonderful people lent me everything I needed so I could see if I liked it. But they didn't lend me a surf SUP, which is mostly what you see around. They lent me a 14 foot race board. I was encouraged, supported and welcomed in a way I had never experienced before. I was hooked.

After the first Saturday session, which was just a fun, social, session where we worked on balance skills, I spent a week in pain. The muscles in my neck and shoulders went into spasm. I woke on Sunday morning with a headache so intense it made me screw up my eyes and press my chin to my chest. I felt like I'd gone backwards by years. But by the following Saturday, the pain had backed off a little, so I went again. Another week of pain, but the lure of water and sunshine and good company was compelling. I got my own board (an old Naish) and paddle, and started working on improving my technique.

This happened every week. My shoulders would involuntarily rise until they were almost level with my earlobes. My lower back felt frighteningly unstable, as if it would herniate again. It didn't. I took painkillers. I had bodywork with Pete when I could afford it. I was grumpy and miserable most days.

Despite the pain and headaches, being out on the river with fun, adventurous people who love the outdoors was fabulous. Moving through the water without the noise of a motor, cruising past seagulls, terns and pelicans on sandbanks, watching the stingrays dart across the river bed, feeling the warm sun on my skin - oh it was such good medicine.

At some point, I realised that I was only in pain for 5 days after each session. I decided that at the point where I was only in pain for 3 days, I'd start going to a second training session each week.

I was still going to see Pete regularly. It seemed like my body trusted him a little more, trusted that even if the healing process resulted in more pain, improvements were happening. Change was happening. The pain I was in after each session was different week to week. Sometimes I had to go back for a tweak a few hours after a session because some part of my body had gone into spasm.

Weeks passed and I was down to 4 days of pain after paddling. My faith in my resilience grew. I started to feel something I hadn't experienced since childhood: the capacity of my body to bounce back.

After several months, when post paddling pain was down to just 3 days, I began paddling twice a week with the club. We met on the water at 5.30am for 'serious training'. Everyone else steamed away from me in the semi-darkness. I spent weeks and weeks trailing after them. They'd paddle up river until I couldn't see them, then turn around and paddle back to me. I wanted to keep up, I wanted to get faster, but overdoing it just resulted in extra pain days and I didn't like that. So I persisted at my own pace.

Here and there I had a blessed pain-free day. If you've experienced chronic pain, you know what a gift these days are. The dark cloud over the future lifts, it seems like so much more is possible, the relief is almost orgasmic. I held tight to those days. If I could have one, I could have more.

So here I am in my second session for the week, pushing the paddle down into the dark water, pulling it out at my feet, receiving the first rays of the sun on my skin, in my eyes. The arced sliver of moon has ducked below the horizon. If I died right now, I'd be satisfied. I'm in pain but it's doable. I'm noticing the muscles that are developing along either side of my spine, providing support that didn't exist before. I can feel the beginnings of resilience in my body, a tiny but growing trust that change is occurring. There's a chink of light opening somewhere in my being, the possibility of a different life.

NINE – 1983

Maybe I'm 11. I'm at Dad's. There's a girl staying here and she's the same age as me. She's the daughter of a friend of my step-mum's. Is she Canadian? I can't remember. Her name is Annette. She kind of sounds American and she's so fun. Her nose and cheeks are covered in sandy freckles. When she smiles they bunch together. She's very cute. We're upstairs in the bedroom jumping off the top bunk onto the floor. We're laughing so hard my cheeks hurt. I'm sure it's really annoying for anyone downstairs, but no one's come to stop us yet.

I do the biggest jump. There's something glorious about leaving the safety of the bunk, the few seconds of flying. I land wrong and the rug slips. My back foot lands on a carpet tack that's come loose. I feel it stab into the middle of the sole of my foot. I sit down hard and flip my foot towards me. The shiny head of the tack is flush with my skin. Blood is running out from under it and making a puddle on the floor. Pull it out, Annette says, screwing up her face. I feel sick. I've bitten my nails too short to get hold of the tack. The blood is making it slippery and hard to grab. Annette reaches across and snatches it out of my foot. She drops it. We watch it roll around and settle. The spiky part is like a pyramid, a wedge, a punishment.

We stare at the bloody hole in my foot. I need a plaster, I say. I walk-hop out of the room and down the narrow stairs. Annette stays put. I rummage around in the kitchen cupboard. There are no plasters in the place they're usually kept. I need Dad. I leave a trail of bloody droplets from the kitchen to the living room. Dad's slumped in the big green armchair. He's got a book on his lap but I can tell he's not reading it. He looks up at me. His eyelids droop and his chin is kind of resting on his chest. He's drunk. I need plasters, Dad. I jumped on a carpet tack. Look! I show him my foot. He mumbles something, maybe it's Hmmm. His eyes are closing. We haven't got any plasters Dad, I need some. He waves a floppy arm around. I roll my eyes.

My step-mum is in bed. She's very pregnant and not to be bothered with us children. I know there's a corner shop maybe a mile down the road. I just need money. I hunt around, leaving bloody footsteps everywhere, until I find my step-mum's purse. I don't know how much plasters cost, so I grab a tenner and put it in my shorts pocket. I sit down on the mat by the front door and strap on my favourite blue sandals. I like how the thin straps are navy blue but the soles are white.

I walk down the road as fast as I can. My carpet tack foot squishes and slides in my shoe each time I take a step. We're in the grey of central London. It's not the best area, but it's OK. I'm sure I'll be fine. I keep walking and I don't look at anyone who walks past. I don't look at the cars or their drivers. I have my hand wrapped tight around the tenner in my pocket. My foot hurts. I should have asked Annette to come with me. That would've been more fun. Some lady walks towards me and asks if I'm OK. There's blood coming out of the sides of my shoe. I don't look at her either. I look at the pavement and walk a bit faster. I feel sensible. I'm sorting it out myself. My practical, uncomplaining, Welsh grandma would probably approve.

The shop is tiny. The shelves are so close together you almost have to turn sideways to get down the aisles. They don't have enough lights and there are squillions of things crammed onto the shelves. It takes ages to find the plasters. I keep thinking the bleeding has stopped and then I take another step and a bit more blood comes out the side of my sandal. I go up to the counter. There's a man in a grey wool jumper serving, who I don't look at. I give him the sweaty tenner and put the change in my pocket.

I sit down on the step outside the shop and unbuckle my sandal. The blood has made weird patterns on the white sole. Some of it is drying and flaky. I unwrap a plaster and stick it over the hole in my foot. Before I've had a chance to scrunch up the wrappers, I see the blood coming through the plaster. I stick another one on top, crossways to the first one. The blood is still coming through. I peel another plaster from its paper and stick it on. I keep putting plasters on until no more blood comes through. There's an upside-down hill on the sole of my foot. I try and put the sandal on but with the lump of plasters, the buckle won't do up.

Never mind. I'll walk barefoot. I carry my one sandal and the almost empty box of plasters back towards the house. It's funny walking with one shoe on and one off. I like the rolling strangeness of the feeling. I walk on the toes of my bad foot, careful not to put the sole down on the dirty pavement. Now that I'm thinking about how dirty it is, I notice the gum, and the gobs of spit, the dog turds, and blotches of stuff, who knows what it is. Yuck.

The front door is slightly open. I must have forgotten to shut it. Inside, nothing has changed. I make a lot of noise putting the coins back in my step-mum's purse, but Dad doesn't wake up. I check my foot. Maybe the bleeding has stopped. I go slowly up the stairs. Annette is reading a book in our room. She puts it down. We sit with our backs against the edge of the bottom bunk and she tells me stories about where she lives. Every so often I glance at the lump of plasters. I sorted it out myself. I'll probably get in trouble when my step-mum gets up and there's blood all over the place. Oh well. Annette says something funny. We laugh and I watch her freckles dance.

TEN - 1987

I have an evil stepfather (ESF), of the fairy tale kind. He's a captain of industry (apparently). He was the first private in the Marines to be made an officer without officer training school (also apparently). He was a champion boxer. His nose and ears look like they've been pounded with a steak tenderiser. His face is a web of broken red thread veins. He has a few thin strips of greasy hair that he smears across his baldness. His shoulders and back are muscled and bowed from boxing and rugby, but his bum and legs are tiny. Basically, he's a giant red toad. The idea that him and Mum have sex … I can't even think about it without feeling sick.

He's prone to sticking his chest out and

barking things like "I wouldn't have you in my platoon, Girlie', or 'if you're not careful I'll throw you through that window, Girlie'. God I hate that word - Girlie. Makes my hands curl into fists. Who'd want to be in his bloody platoon anyway? He's not even in the Marines anymore. Idiot.

Mum met him when I was 10. I knew from the moment I saw him that he was no good. She had other boyfriends. One was an ambulance man with long curly brown hair. I liked him. One was younger than Mum. He could put his feet behind his head and made her laugh. She married the toad. I think she was worried about how she'd manage with three children and my dad paying almost no maintenance. Apparently the ESF was lovely to her at the beginning. Not now, that's for sure.

My bedroom at home is right above the kitchen. The ESF and Mum are down there night after night arguing. He gets back from the pub and starts raving. He calls Mum a fishwife and a bitch. He tells her she needs to dress differently, wear high heels and tight skirts, that she's unattractive. Why isn't she more like her friend Marie who wears tight jumpers that show off her boobs? Mum tells him that I'm trying to sleep above them. This makes him even angrier. He shouts louder. Night after night, the same thing. Most nights, even when the house grows quiet. I lie awake till 1 and 2 am with my Walkman turned up loud. Sleep is a slippery thing I can't quite get hold of.

I'm 15 and we're in Italy on a family holiday. It's been hell from the beginning. The ESF has all the Italian money and he won't give Mum any. So anytime she needs to buy something, she has to go to him and grovel, and he gets to decide whether she's allowed to buy that thing, and then hand out the cash like he's Captain Generous. Or not. I hate seeing my mother humiliate herself like that, but what choice does she have? If any one of us says anything that isn't about how great everything is, he goes on massive, sweaty, red-faced rants about how ungrateful we are, how it's his money that's paid for everything, how we don't deserve any of it.

I'm trying to stay away from everyone else but it's hard. We're staying in a beautiful pensione in Tuscany. It's a revamped old farmhouse (complete with scorpions). It has one of those edge pools that looks out over the Tuscan countryside in every direction. There are pencil pines on the horizon and heat haze rising off the fields. I feel like I'm in a Merchant Ivory film. This is the possible upside of living with the Captain of Industry. He's paid for a holiday in Tuscany. But any upside is completely cancelled out by him being there.

Every time I put on my swimming costume (a new one in a bronze colour that makes me feel happy) and lie by the pool, the ESF appears. It's creepy.

I've had a fever for the last few days. We're out on the sea in a small motorboat today - some harbour somewhere. I don't know. The water is an amazing blue. It's hot in the sun and the boat has no shade. My throat really hurts. I can feel the prickle of cold sweat on my scalp and back. There are white lumps all over my throat, I've seen them in the mirror. The fever and the throat thing have been happening on and off for months. I've told Mum, but she doesn't believe there's anything wrong with me.

In general, I've given up telling anyone how bad I feel. Doesn't make any difference. But right now, with the boat rocking, I feel desperately horrible. My head is flopping down towards my chest. All I want is to curl up out of the sun in the bottom of the boat, and shut my eyes, but there's a bit of seawater sloshing around down there, I'll get wet. My eyelids are almost closing on their own. We're about 200 metres from the harbour. I can't stand it, the heat, the noise of the outboard, my throat burning and aching at the same time, the way my heart is jumping around.

Mum, I say, I feel really bad. The ESF, who's sitting right at the front of the boat with his chest puffed out like Napoleon, whips around. There's nothing wrong with her, he snarls at my mother, she's making it up.

I just want to lie down. All I want is to stop having to hold up my body. I try and lie on the thin metal bench seat, but with the boat bobbing on the waves, I can't find the right way to do it. A moaning noise comes out of my mouth. I didn't mean it to.

I don't think she's making it up, says Mum. They start arguing about me. Their voices are floating around the space above my head, like I'm dreaming. I feel far away. I can feel my brother and sister trying to shrink, become part of the scenery. My throat hurts so much. If I bring my knees up, I can kind of rest my head between them and put my arms on top. All I can see is the inside of my thighs in my shorts. I can feel the roll and bob of the boat and the burning in my throat that makes me breathe through my mouth. I can smell the sea salt air and the engine fumes. I want to disappear or die, or something. Just make it stop.

They keep arguing until somehow it's decided that the boat trip should be abandoned. We're going back to the harbour. I'm so relieved that I'll be able to get off the boat and lie down, that I start crying. The ESF is in a rage. I don't even need to look up from my legs to know what he'll look like: his fat face blazing red, wisps of hair blowing in the wind, thin lips pressed together, chest inflated. He's raving about the waste of money, how I'm just lying about how I feel to get attention, that I just want to ruin everyone's holiday. He goes on and on and on, all the way back to the harbour. God I hate him.

The rest of the holiday is a blur. When we get home to England, I finally convince Mum to take me to the doctor. He immediately refers us to an Ear Nose Throat doctor. That doctor tells my mother that my tonsils are in the worst state he's ever seen. That I have a serious infection that should have been attended to long before now. There's actual pus dripping down the back of my throat. I'm scheduled for surgery as soon as possible and dosed up on high strength antibiotics. I end up spending New Year's Eve in hospital vomiting up blood for hours after they remove my festering tonsils.

It's some kind of victory that there really was something wrong with me. I want to tell the ESF: see I wasn't lying, they're the worst tonsils that doctor has ever seen. See, you horrible mean toad of a man. Of course I wouldn't actually say that. You never know what he might do. In any case, he's moved back to picking on my mother about her shortcomings.

ELEVEN – 2021 to 2023

I often overheard the members of the SUP club talking about racing. It seemed like something I'd never get to. How could I possibly race? I couldn't even keep up, never mind race. I was frightened that the push required for racing would shove me into a new and deeper world of pain. But my curiosity was piqued. I started wondering … could I? Could I catch up with everyone else? Could I race?

I trained twice a week for months, wrestling with the post-paddle pain, but going back again each week to see if I could. Could I get just a little faster, could I get past that person, or catch up with someone else? I got a faster, narrower board and slowly slowly I started catching people. I realised that more was, in fact, possible.

Pete and I talked about increasing the resilience in my body, bit by bit. At first I didn't understand what he meant. But by experimenting with how much effort I put in when I trained, I learned how far I could push myself without debilitating pain afterwards. Each little increment of improvement without additional pain deepened my faith in my body and its capacity to get stronger, to heal.

I overdid it often. We live in a culture that values winning, effort and having a go. There's not a great deal of space for working with your own limitations, for goals that are incremental, sometimes tiny, that no one else would even notice, let alone rate. I really struggled with this. I felt like I should make excuses for my slow progress, tell people about my injuries, my bad posture, the pain that limited everything. But when I told people, it felt awkward and unnecessary. I felt ashamed to not be able to 'just do it', ashamed of being imperfect. I got myself tangled up in internal knots over and over. It took many episodes of listening to myself making excuses and trying to get people to understand, to realise that I just needed to do what worked for me and that it was no one's business but mine. I didn't need to tell people my issues, I didn't need to make excuses. I just needed to take care of myself.

Internal agonising aside, I received huge encouragement from the club and from our coach. Those wonderful people told me over and over again that I would get faster, that I would improve, that I could do it.

I was terrified before my first race. We were racing on a river I'd never paddled before, with people from across the state. I had no idea what the standard was or how I compared. We had to start the race sitting on our boards. I bobbed around on the clear blue waters of the Elliott River with my heart slamming against my ribs.

When the starter's horn blew, I leapt to my feet and paddled with everything I had. My focus closed down to just the 5 metres in front of the nose of my board. I chased down a guy who was paddling faster than me and rode his wash for half the race. At the turning buoy, I steamed past him and then gave it everything I had for the remainder of the race. I crossed the line red-faced, sweating and nauseated.

I won my age category. I was astonished. I took my glass trophy and grinned like an idiot for hours. I was also in hideous pain for days afterwards, almost crushed by a headache to end all headaches. But somehow it didn't matter because I'd completed the race. That win lit a fire inside me.

I should tell you that I've never been an

athlete. I played a bit of tennis as a kid, but I was no good at school sports and I loathed team sports. It was never my thing and I didn't believe I could do it. I thought I wasn't 'that kind of person'. Truthfully, I never felt good enough. I felt like the wrong kind of person, faulty, and from the wrong kind of messed up family. I would never have been able to wrap words around those ideas back then. I just had overwhelming feelings that stopped me from even trying. To become an athlete at 50 and win my first race was beyond my wildest imaginings. The kid in me was delighted.

The following year, I raced more and accumulated more trophies. I came third in my first ocean race in my age category. I won the Elliott River race in my age category again the following year. I won the over 50s women's races in our club. I became one of those people with a collection of trophies and medals. It still makes me laugh. It's so far outside any vision I've ever had for my life.

In late 2022, I started training for the Australian national SUP championships. At first it seemed ridiculous that I was even entering. It took me two weeks and several attempts to get the courage to even register, and even then I only did it with the vigorous encouragement of a fellow paddler. I'd type my details into the form and get to the point where I had to click Submit, and then close the browser and do something else. Who was I to compete in a national competition? I'd only been paddling a little over two years. I felt like a fraud. I was afraid that the training and the racing would result in crippling pain. I was also afraid that I'd totally bomb and make a complete fool of myself.

So began another journey of leaning into doing more and seeing how far I could push without hurting myself. I learned to really listen to my body during those months. Sometimes I had to stop training for weeks because my shoulder was injured, or my neck was out, or my hip was acutely painful. I learned to not freak out when something was hurting, to trust that it would come right, that my body has the capacity to heal itself if I give it space to do that. If I don't push too hard. If I trust my own process, trust myself.

In 2023, I competed at the national competition in Geelong. I won the over 40s Women's Tech Race, the over 50s Women's 200m Sprint, and came second in the Over 50s Women's 13km Distance race. All the training, the trust in my body, the focus on incremental improvement, belief in my resilience, deeply listening to my body, seeing if I could do it, showing up to give it a try … it worked. I had a result. I was nothing short of astounded.

As I write, I'm training for longer endurance races. There's a woman racing in my age category who I can't beat. She's stronger and faster than me.

It's OK. I don't mind. But my guiding principle is to see if I can. So next year, all things working to plan, I'll enter a 40km race and a 100km race. The training may be painful. The races may be painful (especially afterwards). However, I trust that my body is resilient and can recover, and that I will receive the help I need.

TWELVE – What May Work For You (in case it's useful)

I am acutely aware that what works for one person, doesn't for another. We're all human and similar in so many ways. And yet, we're each a strange and unique cocktail of experience, genetics, hormones, and lifestyle. What worked for me may not work for you. What matters is that you believe in the possibility of improvement, healing, transformation and the potentially miraculous. This isn't wishful thinking. It is not written anywhere that you must continue to suffer in the way you are now. Change is the only constant in this world and that includes you, your body and your health.

When you believe that nothing will change,

that you'll always be in pain, always be living with whatever troublesome condition is bothering you right now, it's easy to become despondent and despairing. It's easy to give up.

Do not give up. If I can do it, you can do it. Allow yourself to believe in the possibility of radical change. It might take days or weeks, or months, maybe even years, but it is possible. It's taken me almost 6 years to reach a point where I trust my life and my body, and I take really good care of myself.

It took me years to find what I needed to do, think and feel to allow change to happen in my body. I hope that some of what worked for me also works for you. I trust that if it doesn't, your willingness and desire to create something different for yourself will bring the keys to change into your life.

So here's what worked for me, not because it's

the right way or a recipe for success, but because you may find something that rings true for you.

Changing your relationship to pain

I have a hypersensitive nervous system, most likely from multiple childhood experiences that left me believing that the world was unsafe, I was unsafe, and that I wouldn't get the care I needed. If pain starts somewhere in my body, my whole body freaks out. If it could talk, it would be saying 'Oh my god, there's a pain, oh my god, oh my god, what am I going to do? It's going to get worse and everything will go to shit." In this scenario, everything in my body becomes tense. Before I know it, the pain has spread to other areas. I start freaking out about how much pain I'm in, and the spiral of pain deepens. As the spiral deepens, I become more and more despairing of my situation, which of course, deepens the spiral further.

Learning to regard pain as a sensation and not a disaster was a game changer. Wherever the pain starts, it's just a sensation. Learning to feel into it and describe the sensation is useful. Does it feel tingly or sharp, hot or cold, is it moving or still? Does it have a colour or texture? Engaging the mind in being curious about the sensation is effective in shifting out of freak out and learning to relax into the sensation, not tense against it.

Trusting the body's capacity and wisdom

It took me a couple of years of being crushed by chronic pain before I realised that my body could heal itself. I needed help with that for a long time - from bodyworkers and therapists that I trusted (a very small number). I thought I would always need outside help. No one told me that I could trust the innate wisdom of my body to heal itself, to reorganise itself into healthier ways of being.

What paddle boarding taught me was that my body knew what to do with the pain, if I could just give it the space to do it. I needed to get out of the way.

I know now beyond a shadow of a doubt, that when I trust the wisdom of my body to heal, I'm creating the space for that to happen. If I'm in pain after a training session, I know it won't last more than a few days, even when it's bad. I do the practices that I know allow movement and change to happen. If I stand really still and quiet my mind and breathe into areas of my body that are in pain or feel tense, often the area will spontaneously relax, or I feel to make a particular movement or stretch that changes how I'm holding myself. Tight and painful places unwind, fascia relaxes, holding patterns let go. I have learned to trust the urge to move this way or that, to trust the intelligence of my body.

Relaxation is key. I have spent my life bracing against pain, both physical and mental. Bracing physically - tensing up around the pain and sometimes throughout my body. Bracing mentally and emotionally - oh shit, here's the pain again, oh no I'm going backwards, I won't be able to do the things I want to etc. Now when I paddle and am in pain afterwards, I invite my mind to relax about it - I know my body will come right. I know if I can relax and allow the change to happen, I'll be OK in a few days. I also actively relax my body, softening as much as possible. I check in with my body multiple times a day - are my shoulders round my ears, am I clenching my belly, am I breathing properly, could I soften and sink down and let it all go?

Learning to trust the subtle signals from the

body about what it wants is an adventure. Every time I've listened, followed what's being asked for, and a change happens that leads to less pain or even no pain, it's thrilling.

Exercise

Strength is a big part of resilience. I built my strength up very slowly. It was a painful process, but every step forward encouraged me to keep going. The stronger I became from exercising, the faster my recovery from pain was, the more resilient my whole system became, the more I trusted the process.

Paddle boarding built my core strength, building muscles that support the injuries along my spine. Vigorous sessions cleared my mind, released endorphins and made me feel alive, even when I was in pain for days afterwards. Over time, the periods of pain became shorter and shorter. Now they rarely last longer than a day. A day of discomfort or less pleasant sensation here and there is nothing compared to months and years of chronic pain.

Start small. Find something you like doing with your body and do a little of it as often as you feel you can. Gradually build up. Find your edges and push just a little bit over them. Just a little. You'll know when you've overdone it. Then you rest and trust that you'll recover and start again. You'll know when you haven't done enough. Listen to your body. It will tell you. It's wise and intelligent.

The frustration is real. I've been doing callisthenics for the last 8 months partly to build strength for paddling. My progress is painfully (pun intended) slow. I had to give up on pull ups and burpees because they create too much pain in my neck. I'm determined to see if I can handstand by my next birthday. I do the exercises. Something hurts. I stop for a while. I try again. I'm kind and gentle with myself. I trust my body. I know I need to do everything at my own pace, no matter how frustrating it feels. Sometimes I think nothing is changing, I'm not improving. Sometimes I notice I'm stronger and more flexible. It's very slow, but it's happening, and it's OK.

Give yourself permission to ignore what others might say about the way you are exercising. I remember being at a training session where I knew I couldn't do anymore without really paying for it the next day. So I stopped the sprints we were doing. Someone called out 'come on! Keep on going, you can do it!'. When I didn't continue, that person made a disparaging remark. Years ago, that would have bothered me. Now, I 100% prioritise my own knowing about how far and how much I can do, over anyone else's opinions. They're not in my body, they don't know my journey. I am responsible for doing as little or as much as feels right from day to day. If there's anything in the world that only you have jurisdiction over, it's your body.

What you eat

No one wants to talk about diet. In my experience, it makes a huge difference. When I cut out grains and sugar, my chronic pain levels dropped hugely. You can Google 'carbohydrates and inflammation' and read all about it. For the last year, I've eaten a diet that puts me into ketosis because it works right now for my body. It may work for you, it may not.

So much of what we've been taught about diet is nonsense, and everyone has an opinion about what you should be eating to 'fix' yourself. You need to find what works for your body. I know it can be overwhelming trying to work out what's right for you. One of the easiest ways to start is to really notice how you feel after you eat. Do you feel energised by what you've eaten? Or do you feel suddenly tired? If you're craving a certain food and then you eat it, how do you feel in the few minutes after, in the hours after? How do you feel physically, mentally, emotionally? How do you feel the next day?

There are evangelists out there for every system of eating - paleo, vegan, keto, intermittent fasting, high protein. They'll passionately tell you that the method they recommend is THE one to follow, that it will sort out all your problems. It may. It may not. There's nothing wrong with trying things. What matters is that you listen to your own body, pay attention to how you feel and adjust as needed. Your body knows what it needs.

Care and kindness are required with diet too. If you've been in pain for years, it may take significant time until you see positive changes in your body when you change your diet. That doesn't mean there's something wrong with you. You need to work with your own system, your own body's intelligence, your own internal wisdom and guidance system.

Can I?

This is the question I constantly ask myself. Can I do two paddleboard sessions a week? Can I do three? Can I beat my last time? Can I beat that person? Can I win that race? Can I place? Can I do endurance races? Can I handstand?

Sometimes I can't and that's OK. I keep asking the question anyway. When I can't, I scale back what I'm asking of myself to something more achievable. Maybe I can't do three sessions a week right now. So I'll keep building resilience by doing two until I feel ready to see if I can do three again.

Can I? is a wonderful question because it's always just an exploration. There's no pressure, you're just seeing if you can, for your own interest or entertainment. When you ask 'can I' and you discover that you can, it's endlessly delightful, especially if you've come from a background of chronic pain or suffering of some kind. When you ask 'can I' and discover that right now, you can't, that's OK too. You can ask yourself 'what do I need right now to support myself?'

Maybe you need rest, or nourishment, or to let it all go for a few days or a week or two, and just chill out. All the answers are within you. The more you listen for them and follow the wisdom arising from you, the more the wisdom comes and the more you trust yourself and your process.

There Are Shit Days

When I did the research for this book, many people asked 'what do you do on the bad days?'.

How brilliant would it be if there weren't bad days? But life is all the things, so there are bad days and truly, they suck. The trick, when a bad day rolls up, is to not believe any negative stories your mind is telling you about the future. It might say 'well now you're screwed, you're going to be like this forever, you've had every kind of treatment and you're still in pain - nothing is ever going to work again, it's all downhill from here' and so on. Your mind is not telling you the truth.

My personal take on why it's not telling the truth is this. For those of us who did not receive complete love and care as children (and even the most well meaning parent can be busy, stressed and not paying attention), it's easy to internalise the idea that the world is a place where our needs aren't met, potentially unsafe, and that when bad things happen, we're on our own, and also possibly to blame. As children, we didn't have the inner resources, resilience or know-how to take care of ourselves, so we looked to primary care givers to do that. Unfortunately, many of them failed to rise to the occasion for a thousand different reasons - some malicious, most not.

Children don't understand why they're not receiving the care they need. They make up whatever makes sense to them, regardless of whether it's logical or rational. I know I decided that I had to do everything myself, that it was somehow my fault I couldn't get the care I needed, and that it was shameful to have needs, especially when it was so obvious that others couldn't meet them. This is the mental and emotional wound. It's what flares up alongside the pain of a shit day.

In case you don't believe this, here's a really

innocuous example. It was Xmas day 2010 and my partner and four kids had spent the day at the beach. It was late afternoon, we'd been in the sun all day, eaten a lot, and everyone was tired. We gathered all the buckets and spades and clothes and towels and boys. Everyone climbed into the car. Three of the boys in the middle row and one in the rear facing seats in the boot. The boys were uncharacteristically quiet on the drive home. No one said a word - they were exhausted.

Twenty minutes later, we pulled into our driveway, and I had a sudden pang. Where was my number two boy? My eldest leaned over and looked in the back. He's not here. We'd left him behind. Oh my god. We'd left my 7 year old down at the beach. I'd thought he was in one of the boot seats. No, he was alone, at dusk, in town, on Xmas day.

I gave my partner rushed instructions to call everyone we knew in town, the police, anyone he could think of. I turfed the other kids out of the car and then drove like the proverbial bat out of hell back to town. A drive that usually took twenty minutes, took twelve. Luckily it was Xmas day afternoon and the roads were quiet.

I was a few kilometres from where we'd left my boy, when a car flashed its lights at me. Without thinking, I pulled over. They also pulled over and my lad got out of the car. A random, kind human had found my boy wandering the streets. He'd offered to drive him home. My boy recognised my car.

I put my lad in the back of my car, climbed into the back seat with him, wrapped my arm around his shoulder and burst into tears. I got the whole story out of him. He'd gone to get changed in the shed near the beach. When he came back, we were driving away. He waved but we didn't see him. He didn't know what to do. So he started walking. He met a very tall Greek man who was in town on holiday. They went back to the Greek man's house so he could tell his huge extended family that he was taking this little boy home. You might imagine my horror at this story and what could have happened, but my boy said he knew the man was ok.

At the end of his story he said, I thought you left me behind on purpose. That broke my heart. I spent the next half an hour trying to convince him that it was a terrible mistake. That we thought he was with us. He remained only half convinced. I spent years trying to persuade him how loved he was.

There was no alcohol and no abuse involved in that example. Since that happened, I've met many competent parents from big families who have accidentally left a child behind somewhere. It's a horrible thing for everyone. If a well loved and cared for child, who was accidentally left behind on Xmas day, can conclude that they were deliberately abandoned, imagine what children who live with addicts, or experience neglect or abuse can come up with.

When you're having a shit pain day, it's easy to slip into the woundedness that was created by not having your needs met as a child. That woundedness doesn't understand that there is an adult you, who knows how to take care of you and give you what you need. That woundedness needs your adult compassion, kindness and love. It needs your care.

What I used to do on shit pain days was panic, despair, cry, hope someone would rescue me, feel sorry for myself, eat a lot of chocolate, take pain relief, cry, get stoic and tell myself to toughen up, blame myself for not being more resilient, panic, cry, etc.

I still eat chocolate and take pain relief if I really can't find any physical comfort. I move in some circles where taking pain relief is frowned on - apparently I should use homoeopathy or mind control or relaxation. But I know that some bad days are too bad - that my mind can't handle what's going on and I just need the pain to stop long enough for me to get back on an even keel. On those days, I take painkillers and I don't beat myself up about it. I do whatever I need to, to get through the bad day, knowing that tomorrow will be different.

Side note: beating yourself up about anything only ever leads to more pain, whether it's physical or emotional. It's not worth it.

What I've also found is that when I take pain relief, I interrupt the spiral of pain, where everything tightens up in reaction to the pain, creating more pain. When that spiral is interrupted, there's space for my body to adjust itself. Many times, I've taken pain relief and found that the pain has gone when the painkillers wear off. That doesn't mean that the pain was imaginary. It means that I found a way to interrupt the spiral of tension.

The key for me is trusting my body to heal itself and trusting that I know what's best for me. It's taking care of my woundedness, not believing the dismal lies about the future spun by my mind, understanding that the child in me is panicking, remembering that I can actually take care of myself. The biggest risk for me on bad days is going into old patterns of believing that my needs won't get met, that no one can help me, and muscling through, instead of giving myself tender care.

For me, tender care looks like rest, really good food, spending time with the trees or the ocean, going to bed early, putting away to-do lists, cutting myself a break in every area of my life and making it OK to be exactly as I am.

You get through the shit days by listening deeply to what you need and giving it to yourself, no matter what anyone else has to say about it. It's your life and your body after all.

The Company You Keep

The people you surround yourself with can make or break your healing. Do your friends and family encourage you? Or does it suit them (and perhaps you) in some way that you are in pain?

Hang out with the people who believe you can heal, the ones who have faith in your capacity. Give your time to people who can be real and compassionate about the situation you're in, but also believe in the possibility of change for the better. This makes so much difference.

I know who these people are because when I'm around them I feel mostly whole, despite my physical state. Conversely, when I'm around people who want to 'help' me because it gives their lives meaning, or people whose pity I feel through my whole nervous system, or people who offer me advice I didn't ask for and who are sure they know what's best for me, I feel like a child - small, vulnerable, and like I need to defend myself. I know I'm in trouble when I start trying to get people to understand my situation by explaining and justifying.

Keeping good company may not be the easiest thing to do, especially when socialising and outings are few because of the limitations of chronic pain. When you change your relationship to your pain, your relationships with others also change. I know I've had people in my life who almost 'wanted' me to be the one who is having the shit time, because it made them feel better about themselves and their lives. When I became more resilient, won medals, and had a different outlook on pain and life, those relationships either broke down or just melted away. It was tough because I was emotionally attached to those people. It also freed me to grow more, change more, expand my outlook.

Interestingly, a deep internal belief that your needs won't be met, may lead to relationships with people who won't or can't meet your needs, thus reinforcing the belief. It can also feel intensely unsafe and vulnerable to receive care from others. I know for me, until I learned to tend my childhood wounds, I was highly suspicious of caring people. I couldn't trust them. I was sure they would turn around at some point and betray me or let me down. And in some cases they did.

As you learn to give yourself tender care, the people you allow close to you change. It becomes more and more possible to receive help and care from other humans.

It's Not Your Fault

Somewhere in the rabbit hole of chronic pain, especially if you have spiritual friends, are part of a New Age community, or have done a lot of personal development work, the worm of blame will appear. If you've done personal development work, you will have encountered 'you create your reality with your thoughts', or 'you are entirely responsible for your reality' or 'some part of you wants what you are experiencing', or something similar. It's very easy to blame yourself for somehow creating or desiring your chronic pain scenario. If you could just get control over your thoughts, maybe the pain would go away. If you could just take even more responsibility for everything that's happened in your life, the pain might go away. If you could just admit to yourself that you secretly desire the miserable scenario you are experiencing, the pain might go away.

This kind of thinking is deeply unhelpful because you are blaming yourself, and more specifically, the wounded parts of yourself, for what's happening. It is true that everything you have experienced in your life has brought you to this point. It's not true that it's your fault you're in pain. You are not to blame. You have not 'done this to yourself'.

It can get very complex and very confusing to go down these rabbit holes (or even write about them). The simplest way to deal with this kind of thinking when it arises is to practice profound compassion for yourself. Not just for you now, but for all the previous versions of yourself that have had painful experiences, or made poor decisions, or acted in ways that you regret or would never do now. Life is all the things. There are shit parts and beautiful parts and everything in between. You have done your best with what you had at every stage in your life. If that wasn't true, you wouldn't be reading this book.

A pain body is woven over time and it takes time to unravel it and remake it. This is a work of tenderness, compassion, kindness and patience. Blame, like shame, is crippling, and leads to more pain - both emotional and physical. You have enough on your plate dealing with the pain you already have. There's no need to add to it.

Personally, I talk to the parts of me that are afraid it's all my fault, or that I have somehow done something to 'deserve' the pain I'm in. I know what the child in me wanted and needed. She wanted someone to say 'it's all going to be OK'. She needed someone to take responsibility for her and take care of her. She needed kindness. She needed active love, the kind of love that runs a warm bath, makes a cup of tea, creates a nourishing meal, reads a gentle story, tells her it will all be OK.

I have photos of myself as a child and teenager pinned to my wardrobe door. I used to be unable to even glance at those photos (when they were in albums) without feeling deep discomfort, shame, and sometimes even disgust. I blamed that child / teenager (myself) for all of the crap that happened in my adult life. I felt that she was responsible because she was so messed up by the experiences she had growing up. Realising that I was blaming myself for everything was a revelation. It seems obvious, but I started to understand that none of the things that happened were actually her/my fault. There were adults in those situations who were coping with life the best they could, and they were, at times, incompetent care givers. None of that was my fault.

Now I tell the girl in the photos that I love her. I tell her it's going to be OK, that actually my life is much more than OK, it's mostly wonderful. I tell her I'm proud of her adventurous spirit and capacity. I can look at those photos with genuine love and affection. I'm able to see what a courageous and resilient girl she was. It's an amazing reframe to have discovered her remarkable ability to care for herself and others. I admire her tenacity and gumption. When I look at that child that was me, I have nothing but compassion, love and admiration. It's made a huge difference to my life to have come to peace with myself in this way.

What, you might ask, does this have to do with pain? There are plenty of books out there about this, if you want explanations. For me, coming to peace with my childhood experiences and learning to love myself, made a huge difference to my capacity to trust my body and my life. The resilience, intelligence, and capacity were there all along. That trust helped me to relax and stop catastrophising when pain arrived, which in turn reduced stress and tension, allowing some of the pain patterns to unwind.

Get the Help You Need

Unravelling chronic pain is a process. Some people find a therapist or practitioner who can help them immediately. My process wasn't that simple. I tried so many things, so many therapists. Often they made the pain worse. I felt ashamed that my body didn't respond in the ways they expected. I felt ashamed that I was 'difficult'. I felt obligated to 'get better' so that the practitioner could feel useful, and like they were able to help. I took responsibility for their feelings and self-esteem. I spent a lot of money, much of it unnecessarily, because I persisted with treatments that my body intelligence knew weren't working, out of misplaced loyalty to the therapist.

What I learned from those experiences was, once again, to trust myself. I learned to try different things and to ditch them if they either felt wrong, or didn't work. I also learned to let go of the things that did work when I outgrew them.

Sometimes you find a therapy or practitioner that brings enormous relief from pain, or genuine change in your situation. It's really important to give yourself permission to let that go when it's either stopped working or you want to move on. You owe your practitioner nothing, except maybe gratitude (and even that is your choice).

I have also learned to ask life for the help I need and then be alert for what crosses my path. Sometimes I get an intuitive hit to try a particular person or therapist. Sometimes I'll be thinking about a symptom and I'll repeatedly see an ad for the same supplement. Sometimes someone will directly tell me about something that's worked for them. Life is always trying to support us. We just need to be awake to that, which may take a reframe … which leads me to …

Mindset – Reframing

I know only too well how profoundly aggravating it is to be told to change your mindset when you're in the depths of pain or illness. I'm not even sure it's possible at those times. What's needed then is tenderness and care, from yourself if no one else is available.

At the same time, the way you think about your life has a massive effect on how you feel about whatever is going on.

Many of us are given diagnoses from medical doctors that are very absolute. "You will have to learn to live with this", "there's no cure", "we'll just have to manage the symptoms from now on". It can be deeply disheartening to be told that the condition that is causing you so much misery is something you now have to live with, potentially forever. But you are not obliged to believe the doctors. You may choose to take the medication they prescribe, or the surgery, or the rehab, but you do not need to take their prognosis for your future. That's in your hands.

Good days are your opportunity to reframe.

Most of us acquired desperately limiting beliefs during childhood. Beliefs that tell us we can't have what we want, or that no one cares about us, that we're not important, that we're not enough, that we're powerless. How you acquired them isn't in the scope of this little book; there are literally thousands of books and therapists out there to help with that. What matters is that you accept that you have some limiting beliefs and that they're likely contributing to your pain levels.

There is no panel of judges sitting in the sky saying "Well, Joe and Nancy and Cindy can have what they want, but not you!" "Mark and Michael and Samantha will get their needs met, but not you!". It's nonsense. The beliefs you've acquired are just scaffolding in your consciousness. You can take them down and create a different framework to hang your life off.

For example, on good days, you can spend at least some time imagining what you actually want in your life. Maybe you want to be pain free. What would that feel like? What would you be doing? How would you be living? You can imagine that somewhere in the quantum field of reality the pain-free version of you exists and they're doing whatever you imagined. You can imaginatively step into and embody that version of you and let yourself really feel how that would feel. If you truly allow yourself to feel those feelings on a regular basis, you will start to have a different experience in your life.

If you don't use at least a small portion of time on the good days dedicating yourself to feeling different feelings, you will be at the mercy of whatever scaffolding was built in your psyche during your childhood. And you already know what that looks and feels like.

Of course you don't need to imagine you'll be winning races (I certainly didn't), but you can if that's what you truly desire.

Use the good days.

RESOURCES

Below are some of the many things that helped me along the way. They are offered here because they may hold medicine for you. None of the links are affiliate links and I don't benefit from you checking them out.

Inner Child Work

I found Nate Postlethwait's inner child course to be a critical part of my healing. Nate has excellent resources on his website and also runs an online healing community. You can find his work at www.natewrites.com

Ortho-bionomy

Ortho-bionomy is gentle, non-invasive bodywork created by a Canadian osteopath. It helps the body to help itself. As someone who is highly sensitive and has a nervous system that freaks out easily, I find it very useful, both for recovery from chronic symptoms and for dealing with acute sports injury. Find out more at:

www.ortho-bionomy.org.au

Relaxation

Sarah McCrum is an author, educator and innovator who spent 22 years training with Chinese energy masters. I've found her relaxations incredibly grounded and practical, especially when dealing with physical pain. They've helped me to stop bracing against physical and emotional pain, and relax my entire system. This has allowed patterns of holding that increase physical pain to unwind, as well as helping me to just chill the hell out about life. Discover Sarah's work at

www.sarahmccrum.com

Diet, sunshine & ketosis

Dr Courtney Hunt has worked tirelessly to share information about the impact of sunlight and ketosis on a myriad of symptoms. Following her methodology helped me to understand and clear allergies and brain fog, as well as become much more physically active and engaged with my life. Her on-demand webinars are available on her website here: www.courtneyhuntmd.com

A Note On the Memories

The memories in this book were included to convey in a visceral way the kinds of experiences that contributed to creating my pain body. All of them actually happened. Whether the details are exactly as it unfolded, who knows - memory is unreliable. However, the emotional experience of those incidents is still vivid in my body if I feel for it. Perhaps you have memories that still have an emotional imprint in your body?

I have found peace with almost every memory in this book, mostly through doing the inner child work of Nate Postlethwait (link above).

I am also at peace with my parents. I love both of them and have learned to have compassion for their journeys. I have done my best as a parent not to repeat the behaviours that created so much havoc, pain and heartache in my childhood. I have, no doubt, screwed up in multiple ways, but I've done my best.

We are all interconnected. Even if you have no spiritual beliefs, we are all atoms, protons and neutrons - we're made of the same stuff. It seems logical that the more compassion and forgiveness we offer ourselves and the people in our lives, the more compassion and forgiveness there is in the field of atoms, protons and neutrons that makes up reality. And that, surely, leads to less pain and suffering all round, and potentially a whole lot of joy.

I wish that for you.

Gratitude

This book was birthed through the encouragement of many friends. Special thanks to Eleanor Young and Rebecca Lefton for reading my first draft, giving me thoughtful, supportive feedback, and for being such dearly beloveds in my life. Thank you also to Jerry Jackson, my editor, for his deeply touching first round of feedback. I really needed that.

Thank you to Jenny Blyth for your steadfast care and support when I have needed it most - you are a blessing to so many. Thank you to Rob Rich for patiently working with my body until the longed-for changes eventually arrived.

Huge thanks to everyone in the Sunshine Coast SUP Club for your encouragement, and in particular to Dyllan Constable, whose vibrant enthusiasm, care, and spirited coaching helped me to paddle in ways I never dreamed were possible.

Lastly, always and forever, thank you to my four bright sons, who are endlessly supportive of all my creative endeavours. You are the light of my life.

About the Author

Pollyanna is dedicated to seeing the Earth thriving. She's a writer, singer, dancer and racer of stand up paddleboards (as you now know). She lives in Queensland, Australia with her youngest son. She is the author of the award-winning book, *The Relationship Revelation*, and the children's book, *Heartwood*.

www.pollyannadarling.com